The
True
Heart
of
Yaidron

HS Press

THE
TRUE
HEART
OF
YAIDRON

GUIDELINES FOR HUMANKIND
SUFFERING FROM
THE CORONAVIRUS

RYUHO OKAWA

HS PRESS

Copyright © 2021 by Ryuho Okawa
English translation © Happy Science 2021
Original title: *Yaidron no Honshin*
-Corona Ka de Kurushimu Jinrui eno Shishin-
HS Press is an imprint of IRH Press Co., Ltd.
Tokyo
ISBN 13: 978-1-943928-04-0
ISBN 10: 1-943928-04-5
Cover Image: Triff/Shutterstock.com

The opinions of the space being in this book do not necessarily reflect those of Happy Science Group. For the mechanism behind spiritual messages, see the end section.

Contents

Preface 11

The True Heart of Yaidron
Guidelines for Humankind Suffering from the Coronavirus

1 **Conveying the Heart of Space-Being Yaidron to the People of Earth** 16

2 **How Does Earth Appear to Him Now at the Conclusion of Year 2020?**

   Terrible Conditions of the Coronavirus Could Spread in the Year 2021 18

   Humankind, Itself, Should Investigate the Cause and Actualize World Justice 23

   Humankind Needs to Acknowledge that Its Level of Civilization Is Still in the Middle of Progress 26

   What Humankind that Is Marching Toward Mass Suicide Should Realize 28

3 **International Political Crises Will Erupt from the Coming Changes**

   The Frailty of American Democracy that the U.S. Presidential Election Showed 31

   Mr. Biden Keeps Walking Toward the Worst Scenario 35

The Possibility that China-Russia Relations Will
Strengthen and Japan Will Become the Battleground of
War Has Increased 37

China Is Waging Total War to Destroy America, the
Central Leader of the Free World 40

When the World Falls into Confusion, What Can You
Do? That Is the Question 42

The Current Japanese Administration Will Get Dissolved
Miserably in the Middle of the Coronavirus Crisis and a
Downturned Economy 45

4 Beijing Wants to Revive a Global Chinese Empire Using Chinese Warring-Strategies

Beijing Is Trying to Destroy Even the Emerging
World Powers 47

The Hidden Intention behind Isolating the U.K. Using
the Coronavirus Crisis 50

An Unthinkable Scale of Mass Indiscriminate
Attacks Could Occur that Goodwilled People
Wouldn't Imagine 51

China's Method of Ruling Other Races Is Out of the
Question in Advanced Countries 57

Beijing Is Manipulating Numbers to Make Its Inflation
Seem Like Economic Growth 60

Beijing Is Reviving 2,000-Year-Old
Warring Strategies 64

Japan Will Get Taken Over through So-Called
Coronavirus Measures and Economic Measures 67

Japan Will Likely Get Invited to a Tripartite Alliance with China and Russia	69
There Could Be a First Movement in a Decade to Establish the Bad Kind of Japanese Administration	72
America Could Become Taken Over By an Actual Communist Leader	74
Atheism Is Progressing Even Further in Japan and Beijing Wants the New Emperor to Visit Beijing	76

5 The Crisis of Humankind that the Carbon Emissions War Will Bring

The Path to a Worldwide Great Depression after the Virus War	80
Only China, Who Is Not Following Its Public Promise and Will Continue Carbon-Energy Use, Will Survive	83
Eliminating Carbon Emissions Will Lead to Global Desertification and Global Warming	85
Humankind that Is Losing Religious Faith, Awareness of the Universe, and the Intelligence to Recognize What's Justice Is in Crisis	88

6 What Is Needed to Destroy the Evil Empire

The Belief that China Will Save the World Could Spread	91
Leaders Should Have Made Communist China Collapse Simultaneously with the Soviet Union	94
Chinese People Now Aren't Aware of Mao Zedong's History of Mass Massacres	96

The Power of Ahriman Who Fought the God of Light in
Ancient Times Has Entered Beijing 98

China Will Collapse When Its Global Crimes
Get Exposed 100

Think About the Future Wealth of Nations Under Faith
in God 102

7 **Master Okawa's Concluding Comments on the Spiritual Message**

Resolutely Voice the Opposite Opinions as Major Media
Groups Become Like China 106

Beijing Fears a Possible Worldwide Religious Movement ... 109

Afterword 113

About the Author 115

What Is El Cantare? 116

What Is a Spiritual Message? 118

About Happy Science 122

About Happy Science Movies 126

About Happiness Realization Party 128

Happy Science Academy
Junior and Senior High School 129

Contact Information 130

About IRH Press 132

Books by Ryuho Okawa 133

Music by Ryuho Okawa 143

The three interviewers of this book are symbolized as A, B, and C.

Preface

This is the revelation from space-being Yaidron that was released in video at the conclusion of year 2020.

The contents are very different from that of the Japanese administration and the major Japanese media groups, as well as from the popular opinion of Americans in the US presidential election, and from the reports we get from major American media groups.

But from the words of these summed-up contents, I felt something similar to the words of God who had sent down the Ten Commandments to Moses 3,000 years ago.

If Japan and the world's major powers that share its values believe Yaidron's words, then they shall gain the power to open their futures. But if they ignore his words, then there shall come even greater crises as tests. It's up to Earth's human beings which side they want to choose. There have been countless such situations in past civilizations. May humankind be with Savior.

Ryuho Okawa
Master & CEO of Happy Science Group
January 19, 2021

The True Heart of Yaidron

*Guidelines for Humankind
Suffering from the Coronavirus*

*Originally recorded in Japanese on December 27, 2020,
at the Special Lecture Hall of Happy Science in Japan
and later translated into English*

Yaidron

Yaidron is a space being from Planet Elder in the Magellanic Clouds. His power is akin to the high-dimensional spirits of Earth's spirit world and he is akin to the *god of justice*. His role on Planet Elder is similar to a judge and politician of the highest grade, and he governs the justice and judgment there. He received teachings from El Cantare on a messiah-training planet, and is now a protector of Ryuho Okawa who is El Cantare on earth. Yaidron is a being beyond his physical and spirit bodies, having an unlimited lifespan, and has also been attending to the rise and fall of Earth's civilizations, wars, and natural disasters.

1

Conveying the Heart of Space-Being Yaidron to the People of Earth

RYUHO OKAWA

The other day on December 8, I gave a lecture entitled, "With Savior," at the Saitama Super Arena. It was the same title as space-being Yaidron's spiritual revelation that I had published. But actually, he wasn't among the supporting spirits that day. Because of this and his focus mainly having been on managing security, I felt that he must have things he wants to say. I'd like to find out about them today.

Also, there's a sense that we're on the verge of various kinds of huge, abnormal changes on a global scale. So I'd like to also find out how such things appear to someone of an extraterritorial standpoint.

I don't know if today's message will also be considered a spiritual message . . . Well I suppose it could be, but in August's, previous spiritual message that we held for his book, we asked him questions that could have been answered by just a normal, supporting human spirit of Earth. So, I've heard an opinion saying the real aim of that message had been a little different from that. In addition to that, I'd like to avoid making this a convenient-sounding message to ourselves by asking matters internal to Happy Science. We should ask him questions about how outside matters look to his eyes. These are some points to be careful about.

Now, then, let's get started.

We're very grateful for your daily protection and support. O the space-being Mr. Yaidron. I ask you to please tell all of us, the people of Earth, your thoughts.

[*About twenty seconds of silence pass.*]

2

How Does Earth Appear to Him Now at the Conclusion of Year 2020?

Terrible Conditions of the Coronavirus Could Spread in the Year 2021

YAIDRON
This is Yaidron.

A
Thank you very much for coming here today, Mr. Yaidron.

YAIDRON
Okay.

A

Thank you very much for protecting Master Ryuho Okawa day in and day out. Thank you, also, for giving us guidelines for humanity. As Master Okawa said earlier, during the summer, we published your spiritual revelation as a book entitled *With Savior: Messages from Space-Being Yaidron*[1]. Master also gave us the song entitled, "With Savior."[2] There are people all over Japan and the world who are listening to and singing this song, especially Master's believers.

We've entitled today's spiritual message as, "The True Heart of Yaidron." Could you give us your message to humankind and let us listen to your thoughts?

YAIDRON

Yes. Well, I don't know whether what I say will come true or not. But I'd be glad if you'll listen to what we feel and especially what my thoughts have been as one view with a slightly different perspective on things. I'd like to speak from a standpoint separated from any particular person's interests.

A

First, we'd like to ask how Earth appears to you from the standpoint of the universe. We understand that the coronavirus has spread this year and this situation doesn't seem to be ending. We can clearly see that the world has been going through second and third waves of the virus and that the infections have spread further.

In addition to that, the results of the U.S. presidential election—the number-one country of the world—will get confirmed soon, according to regulations. Currently, Trump is continuing his fight for a comeback, or rather, he's continuing to fight, believing that the results can't be confirmed yet. We feel that these events hold significant meaning to the future of Earth. Mr. Yaidron, how does this situation appear to your eyes now, as the year 2020 comes to a close?

YAIDRON

Well, I'm a deity of the ancient people of Earth. But, I'm not seen as one by modern people. So for the most part, I think it's not likely for human beings to act on anything I say. So I've been giving my opinions through the few channels that are open to me, wondering how much of my words will prevail through changing times.

With regards to the coronavirus, I believe you received opinions from the universe at the beginning of this year, when the virus' spread was still very small. You received the first spiritual message[3] when infections numbered only 10,000 to 20,000 people. Since we forecasted that it will reach astronomical numbers, compared to the rest of the world this was a very big figure to you at that time. And at this current timing of the virus' third wave, 80 million people have already gotten infected and about 2 million people have died.[4] As you've been told since the beginning, I think that these numbers will increase. It's not something that can be helped.

Various countries are currently developing vaccines. But in addition to time being required to verify their effectiveness, many new virus variants have started to come out when manufacturing them started. Meaning, the vaccines that are being manufactured right now aren't going to be effective. Even if vaccines get manufactured for the currently-spreading coronavirus, new research will be required to develop vaccines for the variant viruses. So, the virus' spread will continue in a different form. If anyone believes that the coronavirus will mostly stop spreading and everything will go back to normal come January or February after the New Year, then to your regret, that's going to be very wishful thinking. Therefore, I will say that my forecast for the next year (2021) is that an even more terrible situation will spread.

Humankind, Itself, Should Investigate the Cause and Actualize World Justice

YAIDRON

You must have separate questions on America, so I'll wait to speak more on that topic. But we don't intend to save all of humankind immediately by some way or other. This is a civilization experiment, a time of trial, and something humankind, itself, needs to face.

We've said consistently that the coronavirus didn't occur naturally, that it is a man-made virus having characteristics of a biological weapon, a virus weapon. But, well, only *The Liberty* magazine listened sincerely to and reported what we've said. There were some individuals here and there who spoke about that as their own opinion, based on taking self-responsibility. But because overall disbelief was stronger, there is a lack of unity in the international community. In addition to that, you couldn't influence the American mass media enough.

There wasn't room for doubt in our eyes, however. And we knew, since the beginning, that the coronavirus was man-made, had been weaponized, and that more than one type of it is out there. But since humanity needs to learn what will happen from such kinds of deeds, we aren't going to erase it immediately. The number of victims will grow larger, but we would definitely like humankind, itself, to investigate what caused it. We would like for humankind, itself, to also decide what should be done about the people who committed this deed.

Spiritual Interview

Also—how do I say this—we'd like the people of Earth to take responsibility to actualize world justice according to the decision that they make. Since there are English translations on us that have been published, President Trump of America could be expecting Mr. Biden to suddenly get struck by lightning before January 20 and die. It's not completely impossible that Mr. Trump is expecting this to happen. But if we did such a thing, we would become murderous space people. We don't intend to take any clear action right now. We would like humankind to take responsibility for the cause of this outcome. I do intend to continue offering my advice as the need arises, going forward, though.

Humankind Needs to Acknowledge that Its Level of Civilization Is Still in the Middle of Progress

YAIDRON

Over the course of this year, it's become clear how inaccurate humanity's mass-media-centered public opinion is. You could say that humankind is now in a state of great confusion.

In addition to the mass media, the medical world is now experiencing an overwhelming powerlessness, despite that it was once thought to be the forefront of modern academia, had overtaken religion, and had been the top academic authority. This might be a difficult experience to go through.

But I would like the people of Earth to acknowledge that the civilization on Earth is only in the middle of its progress and that its level of scientific progress cannot deny the existence of God, Buddha, high deities, and space beings.

Spiritual Interview

Japan was overjoyed when its small rocket landed on Ryugu (a small asteroid) and was able to obtain small rock fragments. But there is a great difference between Earth's level and our level that I'm trying to help you understand. The difference in our levels is regarding not just technological advancement but also people's grade of awareness. This being the case, it's only natural that the different levels of awareness between us and Earth will lead to different opinions. You could be happy about bringing back rock fragments from somewhere in the universe that took you many years to get to. But we are capable of doing that in a matter of two or three seconds. This may sound rude to you, but we are watching you with the same feelings as human beings watching ants walking in and out of their nests.

What Humankind that Is Marching Toward Mass Suicide Should Realize

A

You had told us before that when looking onto Earth from the universe, humankind appears to want to commit mass suicide. You had told us, just now, that the coronavirus issue is far from ending. Do you mean that our situation has not changed yet, after all?

YAIDRON

Yes, that's what I think. I think that humankind is trying to commit mass suicide. Something is causing that to happen, of course. For example, a mass suicide is basically the same as a crowd of rats (lemmings) or, according to the Bible, a legion of swine possessed by evil spirits jumping into the sea and drowning to death. Those animals know that jumping into the sea will lead to drowning to death. But when the leaders

Spiritual Interview

at the forefront of thousands or tens of thousands of them run downhill and jump into the sea, all the followers will follow them and drown together. Even though it's obvious that such an outcome will result if you consider the cause-and-effect results, they will still plunge toward that outcome because the leaders aren't able to foresee what's coming. The leaders might do something else, like plunge into the fire or jump off of a cliff. In either case though, when the main leaders plunge deliberately toward inviting crisis to themselves, something about them can't be stopped. In other words, realizing that such action is foolish is itself wisdom.

So, it seems that people believe that the politics, economics, the sciences, medicine, and other fields of Earth are at the forefront of advancement, but unless they see the results of these fields destroying themselves, they won't acknowledge this outcome. Even if they see themselves getting destroyed, they still might not acknowledge that to be true. So, until you

The True Heart of Yaidron

realize your foolishness and go back to the way the world should truly be, we will tell you our opinions, but we don't intend to intervene on Earth.

Spiritual Interview

3

International Political Crises Will Erupt from the Coming Changes

The Frailty of American Democracy that the U.S. Presidential Election Showed

B

You had mentioned, just now, that leaders sometimes head toward inviting crisis to themselves. Currently, people are probably the most concerned or apprehensive about what the United States is going to do after January 20. The whole world is probably paying close attention to this point. Could you tell us what you can see from the standpoint of what you just said?

YAIDRON

Of the nearly 200 countries of the world, America is supposed to be one of the most advanced, but nearly

The True Heart of Yaidron

20 million people have gotten infected there by the coronavirus and more than 300 thousand people have died.[5] This was the situation America was in. Then, as a reaction to that, President Trump was accused of lacking measures against it and for causing such an outcome to result. His presidential race was damaged heavily by this unfavorable wind, the mass media insisted on his taking responsibility, and Americans probably also believed that he should do that.

Meanwhile, Mr. Trump insisted that the real cause is Beijing's conspiracy, but few people believed him, or rather, most of the mass media denied that fact and insisted that the virus occurred naturally . . . China has been persistently spreading the idea that the simultaneously-occurring global outbreak of the coronavirus are naturally-occurring incidents, or that America brought the coronavirus to China, spread it there, and it then spread to other countries. Well, most people don't believe that, I think. But by

Spiritual Interview

spreading that idea, Beijing has made things fuzzy and confusing to be able to see the truth. So, making Mr. Trump take presidential responsibility for lacking measures is one point I'll make.

Another point I'll make is that because he was under that kind of attack mid-election, effective measures to accomplish international justice couldn't be taken. This is a huge point. In other words, Beijing is posing threats in terms of international politics in areas such as Hong Kong or the southern territorial seas and the Senkaku Islands. But the American president being mid-election, he couldn't put measures into action efficiently enough. It was a weak point of the democratic system that was taken advantage of.

Because we had felt the need, this year, to make a military threat of one kind or another against the Beijing regime, my colleagues and I anticipated that Mr. Trump will probably conduct one. But an attack on a black man by a police officer was put into the spotlight. So, instead of reports being made about the crises, there were reports accusing Mr. Trump of discriminating against Blacks or Asians, since he had criticized Beijing. Things got directed toward this sort of an anti-Trump movement and the mass media joined in on this.

Well, America was . . . When we look at these things from our standpoint, in some meaning we learned how American democracy has weakened so much and become foolish [*laughs disappointedly*]. We painfully realized the regrettable condition of the people of Earth. Your people couldn't even . . . We were dumbfounded that you couldn't tell your enemies apart from your friends. The large issues and the small issues were also mistaken for each other. When you think about how the mass media should truly be, we hope you'll self-reflect deeply on this tendency to talk about small issues as if they are large ones, and large issues as if they are small ones.

Mr. Biden Keeps Walking Toward the Worst Scenario

YAIDRON

Mr. Biden will probably change the hard-line stance that Mr. Trump established against Beijing. Mr. Biden will return to pointing to Russia as the perceived enemy of America.

Since Mr. Biden will treat Beijing nicely, Beijing and Russia will end up strengthening ties with each other, further heightening global instability. If a country like China that should be isolated creates further ties with other countries, the world will get split into two.

This happening will lead to a large blueprint for the next world war to erupt. If Mr. Biden brings Russia and China together like that, situations will develop that will make America's victory uncertain if a nuclear war erupts. Things could reach a point that will lead the whole Eurasian continent to get destroyed. If ties between Russia and China lead to a nuclear-war crisis with America, there will be nothing anyone can do.

In this way, Mr. Biden will head toward the scenario that should be avoided the most, the scenario that shouldn't be enacted. Mr. Biden wants to drive Trump into a corner by exposing Mr. Trump's relationship with Russia and so, Mr. Biden will bring up Trump's relationship with Russia again in order to deny his own relationship with Beijing and avoid taking responsibility for that.

So, in spite of Mr. Biden's speech about "peace" and creating "unity, not division," I think that the opposite things will occur. The world will become dangerous, and additionally, the world will further head toward "division."

Spiritual Interview

The Possibility that China-Russia Relations Will Strengthen and Japan Will Become the Battleground of War Has Increased

B

The clearest dangers that develop from stronger China-Russia ties will probably appear around Japan's surroundings, in the Far-East region, including the East and South China Seas. Of course, things will depend on what moves the Biden administration will make. But what level of danger do you see appearing and how should we respond to it?

YAIDRON

As long as the Trump administration will have continued, Mr. Putin of Russia didn't think about or want to have a hostile relationship with America. But in Mr. Biden's case, he's going to make Russia America's perceived enemy…

The True Heart of Yaidron

Mr. Biden's mind is stuck in the days of old. He is a man of the cold-war era of the 80s [*laughs wryly*], so his thoughts are stuck in those cold-war times between America and the Soviets. If he heads in that direction, an old DNA of America will appear, which means Russia will definitely have to . . . Since China's been isolated and Russia has been under sanctions, Russia and China are certain to ally with each other. By creating an alliance of two countries they'll be able to survive somehow. When they do this, the danger is that Beijing will threaten to take control of the seas—for example, the South and East China Seas—and even the airspace. Then, in the name of self-defense against possible American assaults, Russia will try to strengthen its military presence in the Far-East areas, in the areas of the Four Northern Territories to Siberia. Well, Russia's been doing this already, but it's possible that it will put further strength into doing so.

Such a situation means that Japan could get used as a battleground of war exactly according to what Biden is subconsciously thinking.[6] Since Japan will face simultaneous double-front assaults by Russia and China and since it will also become a military base for America, there is now a considerably higher possibility that Japan will become a battleground of war.

The defenselessness of the Japanese mass media and others is sad. The defenselessness of the Japanese Diet and opposition party is regrettable. This is why it's a shame that ties with Russia wasn't strengthened while Mr. Abe was prime minister. He probably didn't understand enough about the strategic meaning of doing so. But in any case, the possible crisis of war is higher now, and so, you can say that replacing Trump with Biden won't result in world peace but, instead, it will result in the heightened possibility of war, weakened American leadership, and bandits.

The True Heart of Yaidron

China Is Waging Total War to Destroy America, the Central Leader of the Free World

C

Just now, you said it's possible that America's friction with China will shift to friction with Russia. When looking at the presidential election, we couldn't see a clear winner. And President Trump has been insisting since quite a while ago that election rigging could have been committed. For example, duplicate ballots may have been cast and there could have been meddling by a foreign country. But the mainstream Japanese and American media groups have not mentioned about this point that much. Could you tell us your view on whether there could have been foreign interference against the Trump administration by the Chinese communist regime? China's communist regime is posing the greatest global-scale threat to the world. From the universe, what do you see about this situation of Earth?

YAIDRON

This is an all-out war that Beijing is waging. The viruses are not just what it's using. It's also stealing advanced American technology, using various political lobbying practices, and everything else it can possibly use. Canada has also suffered Beijing's intrusion and Beijing's activities to set up a pro-Beijing Canadian administration. The Trudeau administration recognized this danger. The UK also certainly recognized it. And so did France and Australia. You could say that Beijing is moving aggressively. Like an army of termites slowly eating away the foundations, it's waging an all-out war to destroy America, itself, the central leader of the free world.

Mr. Biden will probably bring up the Russia-scandal again… Right now, Mr. Trump is pardoning people who were arrested for the Russia-scandal. But Mr. Biden will do the reverse of that. In other words, to stop his own scandal with China from drawing attention, he'll probably dig up the Russia-scandal again. The relationship between America and Russia will turn bad in this way.

When the World Falls into Confusion, What Can You Do? That Is the Question

YAIDRON

Mr. Trump and Mr. Putin—and probably also Kim Jong Un—are the types who prefer full decision-making authority in their negotiations and prefer to judge situations on whether they can trust the person's character or not. So, they don't deal much with people who drift with their surroundings. From now on, after January 2021, North Korea's situation will revert to how things used to be, even though Mr. Trump had met twice with North Korea by holding summit meetings.

In Mr. Trump's case, he had met directly with Kim Jong Un. And because Mr. Trump is old enough to be Kim Jong Un's father, Kim Jong Un felt some trust in him. But now, the threat of North Korea will . . . Kim Jong Un had felt secure that America won't completely destroy his country as long as he doesn't let his threat grow further. He used to feel a level of security about that (with Mr. Trump). But, at the same time, he senses the threat of a possible invasion into the Korean peninsula by China, and South Korea feels this danger, too.

Since China is 90 percent of North Korea's international trading partner, Beijing can "strangle" North Korea to death at any point in time. Meaning, if Beijing invades the Korean peninsula the same way that it has with other countries of Asia, the Korean peninsula will have nowhere to escape.

So the Korean peninsula can only survive the worst-case scenario by keeping its connection with America alive.

If worse came to worst, Kim Jong Un could have asked Mr. Trump for his help and Mr. Trump might have been able to prevent the situation from happening . . . I think that Kim Jong Un feels the threat of Beijing very strongly.

So, there's a lot regarding international politics that can't be predicted until things actually happen. Well . . . things should start to move as soon as the New Year arrives. With the virus crisis appearing globally at once and the hegemonic war progressing, the world won't know what's righteous and what's just anymore. The world will fall into confusion.

But it's going to be difficult for America, the creator itself of this confusion, to right this wrong. The mass media has at least four years of responsibility for who they supported and who they opposed (in the presidential election), so promoting the reverse opinion will be difficult to do. So, "What can you do in this situation?" That is the question. Things are going to get difficult. I think so.

The Current Japanese Administration Will Get Dissolved Miserably in the Middle of the Coronavirus Crisis and a Downturned Economy

B

If that's the case, I have another question. I apologize for asking about earthly-world matters, but since two simultaneous crises are coming soon, a crucial point is about the Japanese administration's, or the Suga administration's, way of thinking. Is there anything that you foresee, especially regarding issues of international diplomacy? Or could you give us guidelines on the way that things should be?

The True Heart of Yaidron

YAIDRON

What the Suga administration is thinking is something you already know about.

Between the time he entered office in September and up to December, his approval rating dropped immediately. So, when thinking about whether his capacity and popularity will enable him to move agendas forward strongly, I think that he's barely capable of preserving his own administration. That is what the year 2021 will look like, and I think that the Suga administration will need to get dissolved.

Basically, this will probably happen because they'll have free time to dissolve the administration because the Olympics and Paralympics will get canceled. But since it will dissolve in the midst of the coronavirus crisis and an economic recession, it will happen in a miserable way. And so, there is no guarantee that a strong administration will get set up afterward. Japan will face very difficult times. It's going to become like a turkey before Thanksgiving.

4

Beijing Wants to Revive a Global Chinese Empire Using Chinese Warring-Strategies

Beijing Is Trying to Destroy Even the Emerging World Powers

B

As Interviewer A mentioned earlier, it seems we're suffering from some kind of mental disease, some desire to commit mass suicide. This seems to be the root cause of this situation ...

YAIDRON

Indeed, I think that you are (suffering from that) [*laughs wryly*].

B

You just talked about how this mental disease will be manifesting soon as various crises in Japan and around the world. In that case, we'll of course need to take measures against them. But on the other hand, we also need to consider what sort of things will happen. One shape that the mental disease has taken is the virus. How will this develop further during year 2021, or from then on? Or will we see other kinds of crises appear? I'd be grateful if you could give us any guidelines about that.

YAIDRON

Well, the current leader of China is extremely confident. I'm sure of that. So, you can see the thinking behind the virus being spread widely in America and Europe.

But the rate of infections has also been high in India. Infections there have reached nearly 10 million people.[7] But the people there are supposed to

Spiritual Interview

be very resistant to germs. So much so, that if Indians have contracted the virus then the Caucasians would have perished a long time ago already. That is how strong Indians' resistance to viruses and bacteria is. To add to that, if Indians are getting infected, then Chinese people should be getting infected also. Yet, Beijing is publicly claiming most of its population to have not gotten infected. The truth behind this needs to be exposed, too.

So, since Indian people have high resiliency to germs, Beijing must have developed viruses that can destroy even the Indian people. Meaning, Beijing developed viruses that were never experienced by Indians before, and it has done this because India could get in the way of conquering Asia. This is the reason why India's rate of infections has been second highest in the world after America.[8] Brazil's rate of infections has also been high.

This means that Beijing is already out to destroy the next world powers that can threaten it and is moving extremely aggressively. I can only think that this person must want to complete his world strategy while he's still alive.

The Hidden Intention behind Isolating the U.K. Using the Coronavirus Crisis

YAIDRON

He's doing everything at once, that's clear. He's attacked America. He's also attacked Europe. And he's trying to isolate the UK. Since many virus variants are appearing in the UK right now, travelers from there are being denied entry by all the countries. The plan with Brexit is for the UK to be independent of Europe. But its isolation will get even worse, now, that infected countries, also, are refusing entry to UK travelers. There's a clear intention behind this that wants to stop the British from controlling Hong Kong. How could the UK send warships to Hong Kong in such a situation? This is a sign that someone has thought through a plan that prevents the UK and America from putting military pressure on the Hong-Kong crisis. But the mass media hasn't realized yet that that is what's happening.

An Unthinkable Scale of Mass Indiscriminate Attacks Could Occur that Goodwilled People Wouldn't Imagine

B
An expert who we interviewed said, aptly, that a single country is waging a global war on all countries, at once, for the first time in history.

YAIDRON
That's right.

B

You mentioned about investigating the cause of the coronavirus. With regards to that, last week, a virus variant appeared in the UK all of a sudden, which you also mentioned. And this morning, Japan also decided to refuse entry to people coming from abroad. It's going to implement this for one month.

The way that the virus variant appeared in London highly resembled the previous virus that suddenly spread throughout America and Europe. It's being called a variant, but when I look at the situation objectively, I suspect someone might have spread the fifth highly contagious virus that was created beforehand.

YAIDRON

You can't visibly see the virus. That's . . . People only see the outcome. People only see the outcome after the virus appears. They're not able to recognize it beforehand. Perhaps you'd recognize it if you were looking at things as you would read a mystery novel, since you would suspect a villain who is scheming something. But if you didn't have any suspicions, then you'd look at the situation from a perspective of "goodwill," and everything will appear merely as outcomes to you, the same way that it appears to the head of the WHO. He is only seeing the resulting outcomes. Since viruses are invisible, people cannot see how the viruses are being transported. But they can be transported through many ways, actually.

B
What you had told us, just now, revealed that the first coronavirus was not aimed at destroying only America and Europe. It was also aimed at destroying India. Based on that, I now understand a lot regarding the intention behind the first virus variant that appeared. Thank you very much for telling us about that.

As you said, there is someone with an evil scheme. We would need to read very deeply into this person's evil intention because I feel that both the general Japanese people and, to some extent, we, ourselves, are still underestimating it. We need to understand how evil this person's schemes are. My reason for this question is that, while researching for the next issue of *The Liberty* magazine, we discovered that 12,000 virus variants of an equal level of contagiousness were developed. But in addition to them, there are 5 other viruses that are far more contagious.

Someone affiliated with the American military found out that at least 2,000 types of such highly contagious viruses have been discovered and of which some were developed by the Chinese military since the year 2012, which is a scary number. If this is the case, does this person intend to spread one virus after another? It's crucial to know the level of harm this person is planning to do and see clearly through his real intentions.

Spiritual Interview

YAIDRON

Hmmm. Your people have the ability of a policeman or a detective who fervently investigates single murder cases. You're capable of finding who the villain is and proving it by examining possible motives, finding people who are benefitting from the death, and examining the victim's human relationships. But cases of an indiscriminate, global-scale mass murder are beyond your imagination. So out of "goodwill," people can't believe that such a thing could possibly be happening. They think everything is just a coincidence, just incidental events.

This kind of thinking is very compatible with materialistic thinking, or the idea of natural selection and evolution. This way of thinking believes that no one created the viruses, that they just "exist" somehow. It's also compatible with the idea that different types of living beings have gone through natural selection and those that survived it are remaining.

The current "one" is like an invisible person going around the world and spreading the viruses. There are 1.4 billion people in China and an additional number of them have spread around the world. That's a number incomparably more massive than the number of Jews and so, you couldn't possibly examine into the minds of every Chinese person.

The problem is that many members of the PLA (People's Liberation Army) have been sent outside to work. They are working at various companies or they could be researchers, or they are international students who are studying abroad. Few other countries are doing this. This means that PLA personnel are infiltrating other countries as actual researchers working abroad, actual university students, or actual top executives in large corporations. They are positioned in places of influence, manipulating information, and actually carrying out murder schemes where they've been sent to.

If they ever leak or confess information that's harmful to China's interests, their families in China will suffer cruel punishment or confinement. Their families are kept in China, which is how a string is always attached to them.

China's Method of Ruling Other Races Is Out of the Question in Advanced Countries

YAIDRON

In addition to that, you mentioned that Beijing has various viruses. Since Beijing has been ruling people of other races who can become perfect samples to test on, it should have tested the viruses on them enough. But this fact won't be leaking out. The people who

Beijing is ruling in Uyghur, Mongolia, or Tibet were probably used as human subjects to test on. There are also other people besides them ... But Beijing could have tested the viruses on the people in its concentration camps and reported that they just died from pneumonia, since that's what the results will show. No one will realize what really happened. Actually, Beijing is able to calculate even fatality rates through this way because they can just blame the people's deaths on pneumonia or the flu.

So, they've already conducted human tests a long time ago, and they should have already also tested various types of the virus. Additionally, Beijing has established nuclear facilities in the countries that are under its oppression, where other races live. Beijing did this so that a nuclear attack by America would result in killing large numbers of non-Han people. This is one deterrent measure Beijing has implemented.

Spiritual Interview

It's a civilization-scale dilemma to have to bomb the very people that you are telling Beijing to free. It's unthinkable for an advanced country to scheme such a thing. To be able to think of such a vicious idea is showing how low the culture of modern China has sunk to. The only source of pride that China has is the warring history and warring strategies of thousands of years ago. That's their sole source of pride right now.

Since Western civilization isn't familiar with the warring strategies of China, Beijing is resurrecting these strategies in a modern way. That's why Western countries don't realize what's happening. What is Chinese warring strategy? It's about deception, betrayal, and trickery. They use such things to create results that exceed their true capability. That is the kind of thing that Beijing is doing.

Everyone had believed that supporting the Tech Giants like Google and others will promote democracy in other countries. No one had imagined that doing so would end up assisting dictatorships instead. This is another outcome that Earth's civilization couldn't foresee happening. In some meaning, you could say that the world inside George Orwell's *1984* is unfolding right now.

Beijing Is Manipulating Numbers to Make Its Inflation Seem Like Economic Growth

C

I have a question related to this subject of the coronavirus. When we look back at the year 2020, the coronavirus crisis broke out in Wuhan, China, at the beginning of the year. Then, this was followed by huge floods and swarms of desert locusts that came all the way from Africa and the Middle East. One abnormal phenomenon after another appeared, and I think that some people in China could be sensing Heaven's Will rocking the atheistic and materialistic establishment in Beijing. You, Mr. Yaidron, are a space being also literally representing the Will of Heaven. If it's possible, could you tell us where these events are headed, how much longer they'll continue, and what is the most important thing for humankind to do right now?

YAIDRON

As you said, China did indeed suffer from floods and crop damages by locusts. But Beijing has censored this information and (talked about) the things that have really happened as if they've never happened, and things that've never happened as if they really have.

Making information public, or, the mass media conveying information to the public is . . . Western countries believe that it's part of the mass media's job to expose concealed information. But that's not the way that Beijing sees the mass media's job. Instead, Beijing clearly uses the mass media to deceive, oppress, suppress, and brainwash its people. In other words, it's possible to use the mass media for a completely opposite purpose (to Western countries); it is being used to control a huge number of people. In other words, there have been flood disasters in China that's also led to many people losing their homes. They're also going through hard circumstances due to increased commodity prices. People are also suffering from a shortage of food. These things are really happening there. But Beijing hasn't reported about them. It hasn't let others know about it.

What's more is that during this tough time of the coronavirus creating sluggish economies, Beijing is aggressively reporting a 5-percent economic growth this year and forecasting an 8-percent economic growth next year. Beijing is manipulating its figures in this way and telling the world to bow down to it. It's telling the world that only Beijing can save the world and so it should surrender. In the world of military strategy, this is the level of using trickery and deception. This is the way Beijing is trying to win a victory without fighting.

It wants people to believe that an economic recovery cannot be possible without Beijing's support. Even if America changed its own figures, everything will get exposed anyway. And so its economy will actually decline tens of percentage points, including Europe's. Meanwhile, Beijing is saying that it will achieve even greater economic growth next year compared to this year, which was at 7 percent. But this is a lie, actually. Pork prices have increased by 8 percent... no, actually, by about 80 percent. So, this rise in commodity prices is actually causing an inflation. Beijing is lying about that and by manipulating its figures, it is saying that it is "economic growth." Actually, its economy hasn't grown. What's happening, instead, is that a shortage of goods is resulting in rising commodity prices. And due to this, people haven't been able to buy goods. This is what's really happening there, but Beijing is lying that its economy has grown.

Beijing Is Reviving 2,000-Year-Old Warring Strategies

YAIDRON

So, a single evil power is controlling as much as one-fifth of the world. This really is the situation that China is posing right now, and you need to feel greater fear about this fact. In addition to that, it's an actual threat against Japan.

Beijing's scheme is to drive a wedge into the alliance between America and Japan by making Japan believe that it won't get any military assistance from

America anymore and that America is thinking only about saving its own economy. Beijing is trying to make Japan believe that as long as Japan continues business with China, an economic recovery can be possible through consumer spending. This will enable masses of Chinese tourists to flood into Japan and cause Japan to depend heavily on the Chinese tourists' industry for income. And this will then lead to China's colonization of Japan. Beijing has already done this in the southern islands. Places in Japan, such as the Ishigaki Islands, have already come under the target of Beijing since a long time ago. Chinese tourists have been visiting this island all the time, leading to increased land prices, various condominiums and facilities getting built for the Chinese people, and them also purchasing land property. This same scenario will happen all over Japan.

So, your enemy should be really feared, indeed . . . Beijing is trying to revive China's 2,000-year-old military strategies right now. This is who your enemy is. What you have been saying is true that China became a world empire only once in the past during the Yuan Dynasty's rule. At that time, China's conquest reached Europe and the Korean peninsula. This means that it had conquered North Korea and South Korea, took over Vietnam, and conquered lands all the way southwards across the continuous lands. In addition to that, China even invaded Japan in the Mongol Invasion, which was the only time that China was defeated. It's clear that something similar is about to happen again in a different way. Yeah.

Spiritual Interview

Japan Will Get Taken Over through So-Called Coronavirus Measures and Economic Measures

B

If that's the case, I think that talking about countermeasures against that will become necessary, I think. If we look at things especially objectively, if America becomes the way that you told us, then Japan will need to think independently about quite a lot of things. Could you tell us any thoughts that you may have regarding that?

YAIDRON

But I don't think that Japan's mass media groups can defeat them. Don't you think so? I don't think that they're capable of winning against Beijing's deceptions. Japanese people are used to harassing other Japanese people, so this is something that they are capable of doing. But the Japanese mass media isn't capable enough to question and criticize another country's behavior.

In other words, Japan has a population of 120 million people and over 200 thousand[9] of them have gotten infected (by the coronavirus) at this point. But if you look at the statistics, not even 100 thousand[10] of the 1.4 billion people of China have gotten infected and this number has leveled off already, in spite of what Japan's statistics are. China's statistics are less than one-twentieth of Japan's statistics, which would make China a very safe country. In addition to that, Beijing is surely going to say that it is also capable of offering vaccines. What this means is that it's very likely Japan will get apprehended and taken over by Beijing through so-called coronavirus measures and economic measures. But I don't think that the mass media is capable of criticizing Beijing about this and defeating it.

Japan Will Likely Get Invited to a Tripartite Alliance with China and Russia

YAIDRON

Hundreds of Diet members during the Democratic Party's administration prior to the LDP administration had spared no time to pay their homage to Beijing and visit it. Such a situation had developed at that time. Right now, Beijing is aiming to create that same situation again. It wants to incorporate Japan into China's cultural influence, set up Japan as Beijing's bridgehead, and create a headquarters and defense base in Japan to counter America and Europe. Then, by worsening and worsening America's situation, Beijing will make America seem like it is the home of the coronavirus to encourage people in Japan to protest against America and tell Americans to go home.

Chinese activists with residencies in Japan have been operating these protests against the American military base in Okinawa. Beijing has always been behind these activists and instructing them. So Beijing will tell them to hold protests against Americans again by saying that the virus could spread from it, and so that Americans should go back to America. From the year 2021 and on, I think that this movement will intensify. That's what will probably happen.

Other than that, Australia is basically the only remaining country that Japan can develop ties with. But the size of Australia is very different to China's; the sizes of their populations are very different. If ties between Australia and the UK and the ties between the UK and America get severed, the situation will get extremely bad. Such a thing happening will require Japan to weigh the advantages between allying with China and allying with Australia.

This is the strategy that the enemy will take, and it's highly possible Japan will get invited by

China and Russia to form a tripartite alliance against America and Europe. But I'll let you know that, if Japan chooses to join that alliance, it will result in the same outcome as World War II, which is defeat.

It's very likely that the Japanese mass media won't be able to defeat that strategy because of its low grade of intellect and overly nice nature. Their weakness is that they're not capable of criticizing foreign countries.

The True Heart of Yaidron

There Could Be a First Movement in a Decade to Establish the Bad Kind of Japanese Administration

B

Hearing about the possibility of a tripartite alliance newly forming is, itself, a strong preventative measure against it occurring, so we're very grateful to learn about that. When we look at the coming year (2021) in light of such a situation and the kind of country that China is, I would like for *The Liberty* to work on releasing information and thoroughly exposing the truth. Do you have any further advice you could give us in this regard? For example, the tripartite alliance that Japan might get invited to join, was a huge word of wisdom to us. Could you give us one or two more advices like that? It will help Japan's future . . .

Spiritual Interview

YAIDRON

Well, Japan might seem to be a pluralist society of diverse opinions, but after all is said and done, it has a strong tendency for everyone to drift in a singular direction. Mr. Suga, the successor to former prime minister Mr. Abe, is heading towards facing an assault within a year. Chaos will follow that. And in addition to that, for the first time in ten years, a movement to encourage an administration change toward the bad kind of an administration will be started by people with ambitions. They will insist that taking pro-China policies is the way to save Japan's economy and to defend the country. Japan's national opinion will get divided again if a minority party insisting such ideas appear, and Japan will become similar to America when people got divided between those who were pro-Russia and those who were pro-China.

America Could Become Taken Over By an Actual Communist Leader

YAIDRON

So, your people have been working to surround China but you could only... There were factors like the coronavirus attack that you hadn't foreseen, it's true. That's one thing. Other than that, there was the Black Lives Matter incident where a black person was killed by a police officer's assault and this... Well, it was the communists who were actually behind this incident. But due to such things, the favorable winds supporting Trump got all completely overturned, in a way. The mass media gave that incident a lot of reporting and news coverage, and it turned it into an attack on Trump. In other words, your strategy to surround China got destroyed by these things, in some sense, so it's important for you to realize that your enemy is working very hard to destroy your surrounding strategy.

Spiritual Interview

In addition to that, Mr. Biden's vice president who is a black woman, is mostly communist on the inside. Mr. Biden also, so . . . If the Democrats win the presidency, well, maybe one year . . . among themselves, they are whispering that he might not survive a full year. Under the surface, there is a movement wanting to increase popularity by placing a black female president in office. There are people who want to be able to say that America is an advanced country where a female or a black person can become the president. They want to be able to say that the champion country of democracy has finally achieved that.

In some meaning, I think that such a thing is something to be feared by the free world, because it will signal the disappearance of the protector of the free world. Yes. Because, this will signal America being taken over by an actual communist . . . due to this trend to overcome racial and gender gaps.

If America falls to a communist leader, what will the European leaders do? Well, Merkel and others are leading Europe. But if America falls to a communist leader, then it's extremely likely that Europe will surrender to China. And the UK is already starting to get cut off. It's a situation that will completely tear apart the strategy to surround China. This is exactly the Chinese warring-strategy from the past that Beijing is good at. And I can see that it's using it to destroy the surrounding-China strategy.

Atheism Is Progressing Even Further in Japan and Beijing Wants the New Emperor to Visit Beijing

YAIDRON

So, essentially, what is important to Japan is to have a set of values for judgment. Japan has virtually made faith in God and Buddha "non-existing." The custom of going to shrines for the New Year ... In addition to that, Shinto shrines and Buddhist temples are literally getting destroyed by the coronavirus measures prohibiting transportation use during the Obon season (the custom of paying tribute to ancestors' souls). These measures are stopping people from visiting Shinto shrines for the New Year and returning to their hometowns for Obon.

B
There's a great risk of (Shinto shrines and Buddhist temples) facing bankruptcy.

YAIDRON
Yes. There certainly is. They (the shrines and temples) are literally not going to be needed anymore. The Obon custom and the New Years' shrine custom will be gone as a result of the "Three C's[11]" getting prohibited, leading to shrines and

temples to close down. Atheism will progress even further as these remaining cultural customs also disappear.

To add to that, Beijing is also out to destroy the imperial family of Japan, after all. Beijing wants to insist that if Japan wants to receive help from it, then the new emperor should visit Beijing. I'm sure that Beijing wants to make Japan do this. Yes. Indeed. Beijing wants to say that it will demote the emperor to the position of the king of Japan, not the position of the emperor of Japan. This is the relationship that Beijing wants to steer things toward; it wants the authority to appoint the Japanese emperor to that position.

In other words, Beijing's only source of an identity is its Chinese history. So, now, it wants to recreate the China that used to be strong in the past. It wants to reproduce the superpower-strength, the world's-number-one strength that China once possessed into this age of highly advanced technology. Beijing's thinking is very concentrated toward this aim.

5

The Crisis of Humankind that the Carbon Emissions War Will Bring

The Path to a Worldwide Great Depression after the Virus War

C

When trying to predict what kind of things will happen next year and ahead, I think that a possible economic crisis is an important factor we should look at. In Mr. Trump's speeches, he repeatedly said that Biden's victory will mean China's victory and Beijing's rule of America. The economy is suffering from the coronavirus crisis already, but he also said that if Biden wins the election, the economy will suffer, and a Great Depression resembling the one in 1929 will come. This was a kind of prediction he made. What can we do to prepare for the possible economic crisis that's ahead?

Also, wars tend to occur very easily in times of global economic crises. For example, places in Asia such as Hong Kong, Taiwan, the South China Seas, the Senkaku Islands of Japan, and other areas are at great risk of this happening. In the near future, what should we expect …

YAIDRON

Well, one issue is the virus war. Well, but this issue was covered only by *The Liberty* magazine. Other places have reported that the virus might have been leaked, but I don't think any major newspaper companies or TV stations talked about that issue. They'll cover news about accidents but they won't cover such types of plotted schemes, apparently. But besides this issue, there's another one. There's one more scheme that's been plotted.

The True Heart of Yaidron

This is the issue that your people and the world have been . . . It's the plot to realize a decarbonized society, which the Western countries and Japan—countries other than China—are involved in. Actually, this is the next plotted scheme to create an economic recession. The movement to create a decarbonized society, to stop carbon emissions by 2050, is the way to the next worldwide Great Depression. This will follow the virus crisis. This is one plot. But there hasn't been anything scientifically proving it, so it's actually one kind of a "religious belief." It's one kind of "faith." There are scientists who have also said so.

This is the path for Greta to become the god of the world. If you examine her mental condition, you'll find psychological abnormalities in her. This is the kind of person that's promoting a "belief" that carbon emissions are destroying the world. Most of the western countries and Japan are . . . Prime Minister Suga also said that he'll completely eliminate carbon emissions by 2050. This will mean the destruction of the civilization if you let this happen.

Only China, Who Is Not Following Its Public Promise and Will Continue Carbon-Energy Use, Will Survive

YAIDRON

China is saying that it will also supposedly reduce some carbon emissions. But that kind of country definitely doesn't keep promises, of course. So then, only China will survive. This is what's going to happen. I'm very serious. Only the people who can use carbon energy can survive, and that's going to be China.

What will happen if this happens? Only China will be purchasing oil, coal, iron, and iron ore. This will give China import power that can bind countries to itself. Domestically, their carbon emissions statistics wouldn't matter to them at all. They'll keep emitting as much as they want. Since they're going to be the last ones to follow the promise, China will survive while other countries get destroyed. Industrial production will not be possible without emitting carbon dioxide so, they'll continue carbon emissions anyway, and they'll be the last country to cut carbon energy. The countries that take the lead to eliminate carbon emissions will get destroyed, so there could be a huge economic recession caused by this race toward carbon energy elimination that will occur after the virus war.

Japan's saying that it will make a complete transition to electric vehicles by 2030. But it is like suicide to say so when Japan is on the verge of losing a way to create electricity. This is just the same as suicide. Japan thinks that that's possible to do ... It's talking about power generation on the ocean, solar power generation, hydrogen power, and other kinds of power generation, but this will spell chaos for all the automakers, train companies, and aircraft manufacturers. What will happen, then? Toyota will make their business more active in China where they can produce the conventional, carbon-emitting cars as much as they want to. Only businesses that can do so will survive. This is what will happen. Only the businesses that have expanded into China and set up production factories there will be able to survive, while businesses that resist China won't be able to.

Eliminating Carbon Emissions Will Lead to Global Desertification and Global Warming

YAIDRON
Ryuho Okawa has said this many times before, but we will also say from our standpoint that carbon dioxide itself isn't toxic. Carbon dioxide is actually

food to the plant organisms. Unless there is carbon dioxide that the plants can breathe in, they cannot assimilate carbon dioxide and grow. Without it, plants would stop growing. So, if you stop carbon emissions, you'll see an increase of deserts in the world by 2050. And when the world's desertification progresses, global warming will progress. You'll see that the exact opposite of their aim will actually happen. Meaning, by stopping carbon emissions, you'll speed up the world's desertification. Green vegetation will die and more and more deserts will grow. This is a very serious matter.

How many years or decades will it take for them to realize this mistake? I don't know. But they will realize at some point. But if deserts appear everywhere, this means that the farming industries will die. Green vegetation will disappear . . . So well, a time will come when there will be no more carbon dioxide, no more green vegetation, an no more rainfall. Since the Earth's soil will turn into very dry conditions, the Earth won't be able to produce rainfall anymore.

So what humans are insisting as being "science-based" or "scientific" is often the complete opposite of what's true. As Master has said, there is a high possibility of a next ice age coming. It's nearing, and we have also noticed that it's coming. Records of the Earth's temperatures have been kept for just the last one hundred years. If this were for the last several thousand years, things would have been better. But because that's not the case, humans are making many mistakes. Earth had been going through an ice age until about 10,000 years ago, and in the process of global warming and ice glaciers melting until several thousand years ago, agriculture developed and civilization flourished.

People right now are trying to stop this from happening, which means that there is a fearful, influential power that is at work behind such a movement. This influential power is what's behind

Beijing. Dark powers exist that are scheming to do such things. And in any case, the path to the destruction of humankind has appeared as the coronavirus crisis and the carbon emissions movement. Then, another path will be coming after that.

Humankind that Is Losing Religious Faith, Awareness of the Universe, and the Intelligence to Recognize What's Justice Is in Crisis

YAIDRON

So, I've said before that humankind appears to be heading towards mass suicide from an overall perspective. This might not be a positive-sounding way to describe that, but to my eyes humankind is heading in the direction of reducing the human population by half. So well, I think that it's possible this will happen.

Spiritual Interview

If humankind stops having religious faith, doesn't want to know the truth about the universe, and doesn't have the intellectual power to recognize what's justice, then we won't have a reason to stop those things. They will lead to the human population reducing which will shrink the Earth, lead to weakening the power of the humans ruling the Earth, and lead to Earth returning to primitive times. If the age of crisis gets to that point, we think that maybe it can't be helped. If you want to cut down the trees and set up solar panels in Japan, then go ahead. But you should realize that doing so will not prevent global warming, it will only advance it further, actually. You need to realize this. You should also know that civilizations that limit its source of energy to electricity to an extreme degree, will be very weak. It will become extremely weak. It's fearful to make electricity your only energy source. Electricity can easily be stolen, destroyed, or shut down. That's a very dangerous thing. For example, it's not that I want to use ourselves as an example, but we're capable of completely shutting down anything running on electricity. This is why I think you will need an alternative energy source.

To my eyes, it appears that humans just want to commit a mass suicide. But even if I say this, only a few people will believe my words... people will just say that we're strange. If I describe what your people believe in Japanese people's terms, it resembles saying that the Japanese race is homogeneous and receiving a response to that refuting, "No, there are also Ainu people among us." They'll just say that there's an organization called Happy Science and among them, a group of people believes in the eccentric words of space people. That's all they'll believe. It's sad to see that happening, but everything is heading in the wrong direction.

Spiritual Interview

6

What Is Needed to Destroy the Evil Empire

The Belief that China Will Save the World Could Spread

B

Since today is an opportunity to talk to you, I'd like to ask you regarding how things appear from the standpoint of the universe. The reason is that when Beijing's evil side appeared this time, I felt strongly that the level of viciousness we've seen has been on another level compared to what we've seen in our past salvation activities, or compared to the evil-ness found on Earth. It's much more vicious.

Is there anything you could tell us about what you see in light of that, when you look at this situation from the universe? If there is anything further you could tell us, we'd be grateful to know.

YAIDRON

The best that the Biden administration can say is that it will operate a human rights diplomacy. Whether this promise is just empty words or whether there will be actual action is something that the Biden administration will be tested on. From the year 2021 and onward, will it use military pressure to assert the need for human rights protection or will it make empty promises? I think you'll see the answer to this. If what you've realized is true, that Mr. Biden has accepted monetary bribes from China since his vice presidency, and this money was received through his son's company, then Mr. Biden wouldn't want Beijing's bad aspects to become exposed. So, when he talks about China's human rights issues, he will probably be extremely soft and lenient. His administration will become Japanized, in that meaning. In other words, his administration will have the same kind of weakness as the Japanese politicians and the mass media, the kind of weakness without the will to take action.

Actually, there is something else that you need to be careful about. You've been spreading the words, "With Savior." But the possibility is much greater that China will be seen as the savior and that this belief will spread as public opinion around the world. It will become an extremely difficult fight for you. There's a possibility people will believe that China will save America and America's economy, that China will save Japan, and that China will save Europe. So, the fight that's waiting for you is going to be a very difficult one.

Leaders Should Have Made Communist China Collapse Simultaneously with the Soviet Union

YAIDRON

In other words, incidents are really occurring in Tibet, Uyghur, and Inner Mongolia, and in addition to that, the Tiananmen Square Massacre occurred in 1989 in these recent times. It's a big problem that Japan hasn't acknowledged making the wrong decision about, regarding the massacre.

When the China-Japan diplomacy was restored starting around 1972, China was very small at that time. It was an impoverished country having a GDP the size of only one one-hundredth of Japan's. Mao Zedong's failure after failure had led to terrible conditions for the people and had turned his country into a huge country of starving people. I understand the feeling of the Japanese industrialists who wanted to help China. I understand the goodwill of the Japanese politicians who had felt apologetic for Japan's intrusion into China during World War II. They put investments into China to help it to grow.

But look at what happened in the 80s as a result of these things. People at that time were always thinking only about the Soviet Union as the enemy. People overlooked China. People thought that they can incorporate China into Japan-U.S. relations and make use of this as a preventative measure against the Soviet Union. They made China prosper and let it become a deterrent wall against the Soviet Union.

The current situation you're facing wouldn't have emerged if the central, political, economic, and mass media leaders of Japan had resolutely called for the simultaneous, and complete collapse of Communist China when the Soviet Union collapsed and the Berlin Wall came down. Today's situation wouldn't have occurred if the leaders had made that decision.

Chinese People Now Aren't Aware of Mao Zedong's History of Mass Massacres

YAIDRON

When the Tiananmen Square Massacre occurred, China reported that 300 people were killed and there were 23 student protestors who died. On the other hand, America reported that about 3,000 people (could have been) killed by military tanks, but (Beijing) took action immediately to conceal everything that happened. Right now, Beijing has erased this fact from its history and has even rewritten the textbooks being used by Hong Kong so that the massacres will be erased. It wants to do the same thing to everything. It wishes it could do this same thing in Taiwan.

In other words, Beijing wants to erase all massacres that were committed before, and so, the real truth isn't being conveyed. The Chinese people aren't aware of what happened since Mao Zedong's Cultural Revolution; they don't know China's history of massacring many tens and hundreds of millions of people. On top of that, Beijing is placing all responsibility on foreign countries. It's blaming Japan. It's blaming England, which ruled Hong Kong. It's blaming America. It's blaming various countries and saying that the foreign countries have been bad to it. It's blaming all of its poverty on foreign countries and saying that China's growth has been thanks to the Chinese people's spirit of independence. In this way, Beijing is trying to spread a Chinese-style justice to the world.

With regards to conveying its own history "correctly," when China had been number one in the world during ancient times, the government had the tradition of recording its own history fairly. But that tradition has disappeared now. And instead, Beijing is censoring everything, including the freedom of speech, the freedom of the press, the right to protest, and the freedom of other types of expression. In addition to that, it's even controlling statistics numbers and everything else. This is what China has become, now. So, if you're not able to expose the evil empire that China is right now, it will mean that very terrible things will occur.

The Power of Ahriman Who Fought the God of Light in Ancient Times Has Entered Beijing

YAIDRON

Also, another influential power is giving power to China from the shadows. Let me think, how many millennia ago has it been? It was probably nearly 6,000 years ago. In the current region of Mesopotamia, there was an intrusion into Earth's civilization by space-beings, by the being named Ahriman. The God of Light, Ahura Mazda, stood up in defense against him and fought. Such a history had occurred before.

An influential power has started to intrude again, trying one more time since then. Ahriman's power has definitely entered China, and some of the people have become his henchmen. Beijing is all based on science-based materialism. So, what they want to get is science and technology. They have no belief in the other world. They think that as long as they can gain technology, they'll become an advanced country. So I think that several beings from Ahriman have also entered China.

If we decide to show ourselves and decide to fight with you, it will lead to a huge space war in the end. So that will need to be our last resort. We would like Earth's people to determine the rise and fall of your civilization with your own hands, as much as that's possible.

China Will Collapse When Its Global Crimes Get Exposed

YAIDRON

Right now, a movement is occurring from Japan to save people. Please make this a power and spread it to Asia, America, and Europe. Work in unison with China's internal revolution and make people aware of the evil empire of Beijing. By doing so, this empire will get destroyed. In other words, telling the truth and exposing evil deeds—the real role of the mass media—will lead to Beijing's destruction. This is how we have been fighting, isn't it?

We have not been fighting by killing people to win. But instead, what's righteous or what's not righteous gets revealed when the truth gets reported. And when evil gets exposed it gets destroyed.

So, your next-door neighbor may seem like a good person. But if the truth comes out that this person is a killer and horrifically murdering people nightly, this neighbor can't live next door anymore. He or she will be put in prison.

If a country is committing global crimes, it is the same. Exposing these crimes shall crush those crimes and that country shall lose international ties, get isolated, and shall not be able to keep going. It will require reforms and to repent its sins.

That country has spoken of past wrong deeds by other advanced countries constantly; it kept talking about them and brainwashing the people. But this brainwashing shall be undone. A space war is possible, in the end, but you shall go as far as you can on your own. There are seeds that were sown already. There are seeds you have sown in various places already that we are praying will flower.

This is why, to fight the evil power, you must get together the powers of the West, India, and other Asian countries by the belief of "With Savior," by the belief that the Savior is on earth. This means that Japan shall not shrink because of your past "evil deeds," you shall not be idle so that evil can spread, you shall not give more wealth to the evil power.

Think About the Future Wealth of Nations Under Faith in God

YAIDRON

You are still thinking of consumer economies to develop your countries, but that experiment has finished. Consumer economies cannot lead to growth anymore. From this time of the coronavirus crisis on, you cannot expect countries to get wealth and development by consumer economies again.

Instead, a different wealth of nations shall be thought about. What is this wealth? It is to start the creation of what's needed in the next coming age, now. The carbon-neutral policies mentioned earlier might create new industries. But overall national strength would shrink as a result of doing so.

So, new industries shall be created from the standpoint of surviving a virus crisis, an energy crisis, or a famine when it comes. You shall think about economic growth by the power of new creation.

In addition to that, that economic growth shall not be one that's combined with scientific materialism, but combined "with faith in God."

By faith in God, the power of enlightenment gets created. And this power is the same power that will take you to the universe. You shall know that.

For your space rockets, spaceships, and things to reach the ends of the universe, it requires time and it's a very difficult thing to accomplish. But in the world of enlightenment, the rest of the universe can be shown very quickly. When you acknowledge this fact, you will start to see the road you should take.

The True Heart of Yaidron

We came here on Earth now because Earth's way needs to be corrected. We would like people to understand about that. In the post-war Japan of now, where there is a lot of materialism, communism, and communism-based science, the time has come to teach Japan the righteous way of thinking and looking at things. If people can't distinguish the evil empire, they should quit the mass media. It won't be a problem if such kind of a mass media goes under and collapses. The people in politics should also stop fiddling with only small things. And instead, they should think strongly, from a macro-perspective, that they will never forgive wrong judgments.

A
Yes. Thank you very much. Thank you for today's precious message from the universe. We want to convey your words and heart to as much of humankind as possible.

YAIDRON

It included some guidelines for your activities next year (2021), I think.

A

Yes.

YAIDRON

You have a press division, even if it's small. So, please do your very best.

A

We will. Thank you very much for today.

YAIDRON

Okay.

7

Master Okawa's Concluding Comments on the Spiritual Message

Resolutely Voice the Opposite Opinions as Major Media Groups Become Like China

RYUHO OKAWA

[*Claps his hands once*] Thank you very much.

There were contents we should watch at the end of this year and the start of next year, I think.

A

Yes, it said a lot that we should listen to.

RYUHO OKAWA

We really need to be stronger.

Closing Comments

A

Yes.

RYUHO OKAWA

Yes, it's very regrettable. But all the major media groups are being operated by people who aren't good. They're becoming like and lured into China. So we will really need to stand up firmly, and keep voicing the opposite things resolutely.

A

Yes.

RYUHO OKAWA

Well ... please do the best you can.

A

Yes.

RYUHO OKAWA

In this condition, America might not be able to fight with us anymore, but I'm sure it will bounce back. Hahhhh [*sighing*] . . . Is Ms. Something going to become the American president in a year? I wonder. Well, the space-beings can't possibly say that they have assassination plans for the president. If they did, we'll become wanted criminals. They definitely can't say such a thing. They could never say so. I'm sure of that. But, since we've been supporting democracy, he's saying that we should take responsibility for doing so. So, we'll have to take responsibility. We didn't fight enough in some sense. That's something we didn't do enough of.

A
Yes.

Closing Comments

Beijing Fears a Possible Worldwide Religious Movement

RYUHO OKAWA

But Beijing has been collecting information about us. It's been gathering our opinions as information and examining them. So I think that it's affecting it on the inside more than we expect. I think that it feels very threatened by us.

A

Yes.

RYUHO OKAWA

Seeing that there hasn't been a huge counter-reaction, I think it fears us. It's afraid of us. Since it's possible that a worldwide movement might occur, it's too afraid to do anything in case the entire world stands up fervently against it. I think it's afraid of religious power. It's having a difficult time handling Falun Gong. So it knows that it will get into huge trouble if it does anything to another religion in Japan.

So, we shouldn't be afraid to do what's right.

Thank you very much.

[*Claps his hands once.*]

A

Thank you very much.

ENDNOTES

1 See Ryuho Okawa, *With Savior: Messages from Space Being Yaidron* (Tokyo: HS Press, 2020).

2 The CD of "With Savior," words and music written by Ryuho Okawa, performed by Sayaka Okawa, and arranged by Sayaka Okawa and Yuichi Mizusawa is available at Happy Science locations starting mid-May, 2021. The digital version is available on Amazon, iTunes, and Spotify.

3 See Ryuho Okawa, *Spiritual Reading of Novel Coronavirus Infection Originated in China: Closing in on the Real Cause of the Global Outbreak* (Tokyo: HS Press, 2020).

4 These were figures as of December 27, 2020.

5 At the timing of recording this message.

6 See Ryuho Okawa, *Spiritual Interviews with the Guardian Spirits of Biden and Trump* (Tokyo: HS Press, 2020).

7 These were figures at the end of December, 2020.

8 This was based on figures reported as of December 27, 2020.

9 These were the figures as of December 27, 2020.

10 These were the figures as of December 27, 2020.

11 The three C's refer to the Japanese government's recommendation during the coronavirus crisis to avoid closed spaces, crowded spaces, and close-contact settings.

Afterword

The presidential transition of the United States of America is about to occur. U.S. National Guardsmen are protecting the Capitol Building as if they're prepared to face a revolution.

The world is being confronted now by the koan (a point needing deep contemplation) of what kind of future it shall imagine when American hegemony comes to an end.

As millions, tens of millions, and hundreds of millions of people are becoming dead bodies, I, myself, have this test of my *Mission as Savior* to guide humankind whose faith in God is gone.

By reading this book carefully, you will get the essential guidelines for this year. It didn't matter who the prime minister is or what the mass media's policies were. This book was spoken from a viewpoint beyond such things. If people choose atheism and materialism and devote to fake-science-belief, there shall come an end to the democracy of this modern age.

Ryuho Okawa
Master & CEO of Happy Science Group
January 19, 2021

ABOUT THE AUTHOR

RYUHO OKAWA was born on July 7th 1956, in Tokushima, Japan. After graduating from the University of Tokyo with a law degree, he joined a Tokyo-based trading house. While working at its New York headquarters, he studied international finance at the Graduate Center of the City University of New York. In 1981, he attained Great Enlightenment and became aware that he is El Cantare with a mission to bring salvation to all humankind. In 1986, he established Happy Science. It now has members in over 160 countries across the world, with more than 700 local branches and temples as well as 10,000 missionary houses around the world. The total number of lectures has exceeded 3,250 (of which more than 150 are in English) and over 2,800 books (of which more than 550 are Spiritual Interview Series) have been published, many of which are translated into 31 languages. Many of the books, including *The Laws of the Sun* have become best sellers or million sellers. To date, Happy Science has produced 23 movies. The original story and original concept were given by the Executive Producer Ryuho Okawa. Recent movie titles are *Beautiful Lure–A Modern Tale of "Painted Skin"* (live-action movie scheduled to be released in May 2021), *Yume Handan soshite Kyoufu Taiken e* (literally, "The Interpretation of Dreams and Fearful Experience," live-action movie scheduled to be released in August 2021), and *The Laws of the Universe - The Age of Elohim -* (animation movie scheduled to be released in Fall of 2021). He has also composed the lyrics and music of over 300 songs, such as theme songs and featured songs of movies. Moreover, he is the Founder of Happy Science University and Happy Science Academy (Junior and Senior High School), Founder and President of the Happiness Realization Party, Founder and Honorary Headmaster of Happy Science Institute of Government and Management, Founder of IRH Press Co., Ltd., and the Chairperson of New Star Production Co., Ltd. and ARI Production Co., Ltd.

WHAT IS EL CANTARE?

El Cantare means "the Light of the Earth," and is the Supreme God of the Earth who has been guiding humankind since the beginning of Genesis. He is whom Jesus called Father and Muhammad called Allah. Different parts of El Cantare's core consciousness have descended to Earth in the past, once as Alpha and another as Elohim. His branch spirits, such as Shakyamuni Buddha and Hermes, have descended to Earth many times and helped to flourish many civilizations. To unite various religions and to integrate various fields of study in order to build a new civilization on Earth, a part of the core consciousness has descended to Earth as Master Ryuho Okawa.

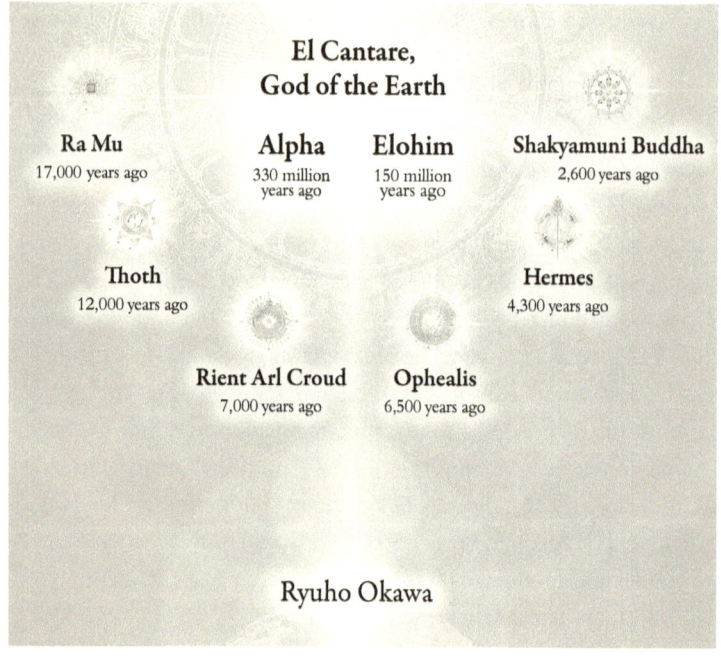

Alpha is a part of the core consciousness of El Cantare who descended to Earth around 330 million years ago. Alpha preached Earth's Truths to harmonize and unify Earth-born humans and space people who came from other planets.

Elohim is a part of El Cantare's core consciousness who descended to Earth around 150 million years ago. He gave wisdom, mainly on the differences of light and darkness, good and evil.

Shakyamuni Buddha was born as a prince into the Shakya Clan in India around 2,600 years ago. When he was 29 years old, he renounced the world and sought enlightenment. He later attained Great Enlightenment and founded Buddhism.

Hermes is one of the 12 Olympian gods in Greek mythology, but the spiritual Truth is that he taught the teachings of love and progress around 4,300 years ago that became the origin of the current Western civilization. He is a hero that truly existed.

Ophealis was born in Greece around 6,500 years ago and was the leader who took an expedition to as far as Egypt. He is the God of miracles, prosperity, and arts, and is known as Osiris in the Egyptian mythology.

Rient Arl Croud was born as a king of the ancient Incan Empire around 7,000 years ago and taught about the mysteries of the mind. In the heavenly world, he is responsible for the interactions that take place between various planets.

Thoth was an almighty leader who built the golden age of the Atlantic civilization around 12,000 years ago. In the Egyptian mythology, he is known as god Thoth.

Ra Mu was a leader who built the golden age of the civilization of Mu around 17,000 years ago. As a religious leader and a politician, he ruled by uniting religion and politics.

WHAT IS A SPIRITUAL MESSAGE?

We are all spiritual beings living on this earth. The following is the mechanism behind Master Ryuho Okawa's spiritual messages.

1 You are a spirit

People are born into this world to gain wisdom through various experiences and return to the other world when their lives end. We are all spirits and repeat this cycle in order to refine our souls.

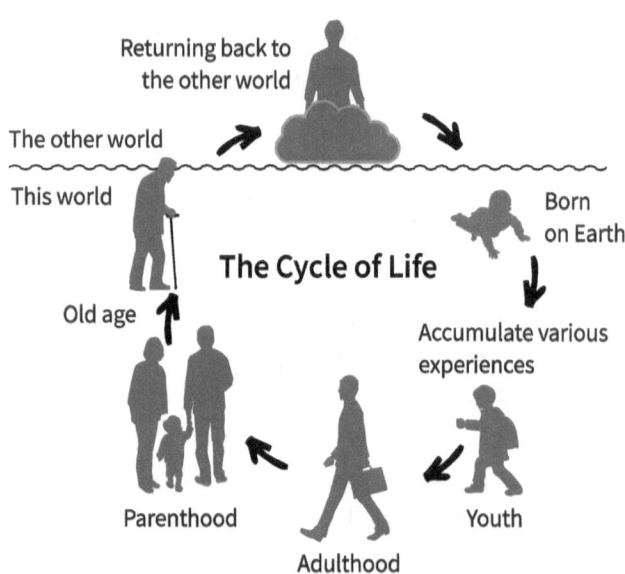

2 You have a guardian spirit

Guardian spirits are those who protect the people who are living on this earth. Each of us has a guardian spirit that watches over us and guides us from the other world. They were us in our past life, and are identical in how we think.

3 How spiritual messages work

Master Ryuho Okawa, through his enlightenment, is capable of summoning any spirit from anywhere in the world, including the spirit world.

Master Okawa's way of receiving spiritual messages is fundamentally different from that of other psychic mediums who undergo trances and are thereby completely taken over by the spirits they are channeling.

Master Okawa's attainment of a high level of enlightenment enables him to retain full control of his consciousness and body throughout the duration of the spiritual message. To allow the spirits to express their own thoughts and personalities freely, however, Master Okawa usually softens the dominancy of his consciousness. This way, he is able to keep his own philosophies out of the way and ensure that the spiritual messages are pure expressions of the spirits he is channeling.

Since guardian spirits think at the same subconscious level as the person living on earth, Master Okawa can summon the spirit and find out what the person on earth is actually thinking. If the person has already returned to the other world, the spirit can give messages to the people living on earth through Master Okawa.

Since 2009, more than 1,150 sessions of spiritual messages have been openly recorded by Master Okawa, and the majority of these have been published. Spiritual messages from the guardian spirits of people living today such as Donald Trump, former Japanese Prime Minister Shinzo Abe and Chinese President Xi Jinping, as well as spiritual messages sent from the spirit world by Jesus Christ, Muhammad, Thomas Edison, Mother Teresa, Steve Jobs and Nelson Mandela are just a tiny pack of spiritual messages that were published so far.

Domestically, in Japan, these spiritual messages are being read by a wide range of politicians and mass media, and the high-level contents of these books are delivering an impact even more on politics, news and public opinion. In recent years, there have been spiritual messages recorded in English, and English translations are being done on the spiritual messages given in Japanese. These have been published overseas, one after another, and have started to shake the world.

*For more about spiritual messages and a complete list of books in the Spiritual Interview Series, visit **okawabooks.com***

ABOUT HAPPY SCIENCE

Happy Science is a global movement that empowers individuals to find purpose and spiritual happiness and to share that happiness with their families, societies, and the world. With more than 12 million members around the world, Happy Science aims to increase awareness of spiritual truths and expand our capacity for love, compassion, and joy so that together we can create the kind of world we all wish to live in.

Activities at Happy Science are based on the Principles of Happiness (Love, Wisdom, Self-Reflection, and Progress). These principles embrace worldwide philosophies and beliefs, transcending boundaries of culture and religions.

Love teaches us to give ourselves freely without expecting anything in return; it encompasses giving, nurturing, and forgiving.

Wisdom leads us to the insights of spiritual truths, and opens us to the true meaning of life and the will of God (the universe, the highest power, Buddha).

Self-Reflection brings a mindful, nonjudgmental lens to our thoughts and actions to help us find our truest selves—the essence of our souls—and deepen our connection to the highest power. It helps us attain a clean and peaceful mind and leads us to the right life path.

Progress emphasizes the positive, dynamic aspects of our spiritual growth—actions we can take to manifest and spread happiness around the world. It's a path that not only expands our soul growth, but also furthers the collective potential of the world we live in.

PROGRAMS AND EVENTS

The doors of Happy Science are open to all. We offer a variety of programs and events, including self-exploration and self-growth programs, spiritual seminars, meditation and contemplation sessions, study groups, and book events.

Our programs are designed to:
* Deepen your understanding of your purpose and meaning in life
* Improve your relationships and increase your capacity to love unconditionally
* Attain peace of mind, decrease anxiety and stress, and feel positive
* Gain deeper insights and a broader perspective on the world
* Learn how to overcome life's challenges
  ... and much more.

*For more information, visit **happy-science.org**.*

OUR ACTIVITIES

Happy Science does other various activities to provide support for those in need.

◆ **You Are An Angel! General Incorporated Association**

Happy Science has a volunteer network in Japan that encourages and supports children with disabilities as well as their parents and guardians.

◆ **Never Mind School for Truancy**

At 'Never Mind,' we support students who find it very challenging to attend schools in Japan. We also nurture their self-help spirit and power to rebound against obstacles in life based on Master Okawa's teachings and faith.

◆ **"Prevention Against Suicide" Campaign since 2003**

A nationwide campaign to reduce suicides; over 20,000 people commit suicide every year in Japan. "The Suicide Prevention Website-Words of Truth for You-" presents spiritual prescriptions for worries such as depression, lost love, extramarital affairs, bullying and work-related problems, thereby saving many lives.

◆ **Support for Anti-bullying Campaigns**

Happy Science provides support for a group of parents and guardians, Network to Protect Children from Bullying, a general incorporated foundation launched in Japan to end bullying, including those that can even be called a criminal offense. So far, the network received more than 5,000 cases and resolved 90% of them.

- **The Golden Age Scholarship**
  This scholarship is granted to students who can contribute greatly and bring a hopeful future to the world.

- **Success No.1**
  Buddha's Truth Afterschool Academy
  Happy Science has over 180 classrooms throughout Japan and in several cities around the world that focus on afterschool education for children. The education focuses on faith and morals in addition to supporting children's school studies.

- **Angel Plan V**
  For children under the age of kindergarten, Happy Science holds classes for nurturing healthy, positive, and creative boys and girls.

- **Future Stars Training Department**
  The Future Stars Training Department was founded within the Happy Science Media Division with the goal of nurturing talented individuals to become successful in the performing arts and entertainment industry.

- **New Star Production Co., Ltd.**
  ARI Production Co., Ltd.
  We have companies to nurture actors and actresses, artists, and vocalists. They are also involved in film production.

ABOUT HAPPY SCIENCE MOVIES

BEAUTIFUL LURE *Coming Soon*

STORY With both beauty and wit, Maiko looks for a man who suits her. One night, she finds Taro, a candidate for the prime minister. Everything goes well as she plans, but Taro finds out that she is actually a "Youma", a foxy demon who destroys the country. What does fate hold for them?

45 Awards from 7 Countries!

For more information, visit **www.beautifullure.com**

TWICEBORN On VOD NOW

STORY Satoru Ichijo receives a message from the spiritual world and realizes his mission is to lead humankind to happiness. He becomes a successful businessman while publishing spiritual messages secretly, but the devil's temptation shakes his mind and...

41 Awards from 8 Countries!

For more information, visit **www.twicebornmovie.com**

IMMORTAL HERO On VOD NOW

Based on the true story of a man whose near-death experience inspires him to choose life... and change the lives of millions.

42 Awards from 9 Countries!

SPAIN
BARCELONA INTERNATIONAL FILM FESTIVAL 2019
[THE CASTELL AWARDS]

SPAIN
MADRID INTERNATIONAL FILM FESTIVAL 2019
[BEST DIRECTOR OF A FOREIGN LANGUAGE FEATURE FILM]

ITALY
FLORENCE FILM AWARDS JUL 2019
[HONORABLE MENTION: FEATURE FILM]

USA
INDIE VISIONS FILM FESTIVAL JUL 2019 [WINNER (NARRATIVE FEATURE FILM)]

ITALY
FLORENCE FILM AWARDS JUL 2019
[BEST ORIGINAL SCREENPLAY]

ITALY
DIAMOND FILM AWARDS JUL 2019
[WINNER (NARRATIVE FEATURE FILM)]

...and more!

For more information, visit ***www.immortal-hero.com***

THE REAL EXORCIST On VOD NOW

58 Awards from 9 Countries!

STORY Tokyo —the most mystical city in the world where you find spiritual spots in the most unexpected places. Sayuri works as a part-time waitress at a small coffee shop "Extra" where regular customers enjoy the authentic coffee that the owner brews. Meanwhile, Sayuri uses her supernatural powers to help those who are troubled by spiritual phenomena one after another. Through her special consultations, she touches the hearts of the people and helps them by showing the truths of the invisible world.

USA
GOLD REMI AWARD
53rd WorldFest Houston International Film Festival 2020

MONACO
BEST FEATURE FILM
17th Angel Film Awards 2020
Monaco International Film Festival

NIGERIA
BEST FEATURE FILM
EKO International Film Festival 2020

THAI
BEST PRODUCTION DESIGN
Thai International Film Festival 2020

For more information, visit ***www.realexorcistmovie.com***

ABOUT HAPPINESS REALIZATION PARTY

The Happiness Realization Party (HRP) was founded in May 2009 by Master Ryuho Okawa as part of the Happy Science Group to offer concrete and proactive solutions to the current issues such as military threats from North Korea and China and the long-term economic recession. HRP aims to implement drastic reforms of the Japanese government, thereby bringing peace and prosperity to Japan. To accomplish this, HRP proposes two key policies:

1) Strengthening the national security and the Japan-U.S. alliance, which plays a vital role in the stability of Asia.

2) Improving the Japanese economy by implementing drastic tax cuts, taking monetary easing measures and creating new major industries.

HRP advocates that Japan should offer a model of a religious nation that allows diverse values and beliefs to coexist, and that contributes to global peace.

*For more information, visit **en.hr-party.jp***

HAPPY SCIENCE ACADEMY JUNIOR AND SENIOR HIGH SCHOOL

Happy Science Academy Junior and Senior High School is a boarding school founded with the goal of educating the future leaders of the world who can have a big vision, persevere, and take on new challenges.

Currently, there are two campuses in Japan; the Nasu Main Campus in Tochigi Prefecture, founded in 2010, and the Kansai Campus in Shiga Prefecture, founded in 2013.

Nasu Main Campus

Kansai Campus

CONTACT INFORMATION

Happy Science is a worldwide organization with faith centers around the globe. For a comprehensive list of centers, visit the worldwide directory at *happy-science.org*. The following are some of the many Happy Science locations:

UNITED STATES AND CANADA

New York
79 Franklin St., New York, NY 10013
Phone: 212-343-7972
Fax: 212-343-7973
Email: ny@happy-science.org
Website: happyscience-usa.org

New Jersey
725 River Rd, #102B, Edgewater, NJ 07020
Phone: 201-313-0127
Fax: 201-313-0120
Email: nj@happy-science.org
Website: happyscience-usa.org

Florida
5208 8th St., St. Zephyrhills, FL 33542
Phone: 813-715-0000
Fax: 813-715-0010
Email: florida@happy-science.org
Website: happyscience-usa.org

Atlanta
1874 Piedmont Ave., NE Suite 360-C
Atlanta, GA 30324
Phone: 404-892-7770
Email: atlanta@happy-science.org
Website: happyscience-usa.org

San Francisco
525 Clinton St.
Redwood City, CA 94062
Phone & Fax: 650-363-2777
Email: sf@happy-science.org
Website: happyscience-usa.org

Los Angeles
1590 E. Del Mar Blvd., Pasadena, CA 91106
Phone: 626-395-7775
Fax: 626-395-7776
Email: la@happy-science.org
Website: happyscience-usa.org

Orange County
10231 Slater Ave., #204
Fountain Valley, CA 92708
Phone: 714-745-1140
Email: oc@happy-science.org
Website: happyscience-usa.org

San Diego
7841 Balboa Ave., Suite #202
San Diego, CA 92111
Phone: 626-395-7775
Fax: 626-395-7776
E-mail: sandiego@happy-science.org
Website: happyscience-usa.org

Hawaii
Phone: 808-591-9772
Fax: 808-591-9776
Email: hi@happy-science.org
Website: happyscience-usa.org

Kauai
3343 Kanakolu Street, Suite 5
Lihue, HI 96766, U.S.A.
Phone: 808-822-7007
Fax: 808-822-6007
Email: kauai-hi@happy-science.org
Website: happyscience-usa.org

Toronto
845 The Queensway
Etobicoke ON M8Z 1N6 Canada
Phone: 1-416-901-3747
Email: toronto@happy-science.org
Website: happy-science.ca

Vancouver
#201-2607 East 49th Avenue
Vancouver, BC, V5S 1J9, Canada
Phone: 1-604-437-7735
Fax: 1-604-437-7764
Email: vancouver@happy-science.org
Website: happy-science.ca

INTERNATIONAL

Tokyo
1-6-7 Togoshi, Shinagawa
Tokyo, 142-0041 Japan
Phone: 81-3-6384-5770
Fax: 81-3-6384-5776
Email: tokyo@happy-science.org
Website: happy-science.org

Seoul
74, Sadang-ro 27-gil,
Dongjak-gu, Seoul, Korea
Phone: 82-2-3478-8777
Fax: 82-2-3478-9777
Email: korea@happy-science.org
Website: happyscience-korea.org

London
3 Margaret St.
London,W1W 8RE United Kingdom
Phone: 44-20-7323-9255
Fax: 44-20-7323-9344
Email: eu@happy-science.org
Website: happyscience-uk.org

Taipei
No. 89, Lane 155, Dunhua N. Road
Songshan District, Taipei City 105, Taiwan
Phone: 886-2-2719-9377
Fax: 886-2-2719-5570
Email: taiwan@happy-science.org
Website: happyscience-tw.org

Sydney
516 Pacific Hwy, Lane Cove North,
NSW 2066, Australia
Phone: 61-2-9411-2877
Fax: 61-2-9411-2822
Email: sydney@happy-science.org

Malaysia
No 22A, Block 2, Jalil Link Jalan Jalil Jaya 2,
Bukit Jalil 57000, Kuala Lumpur, Malaysia
Phone: 60-3-8998-7877
Fax: 60-3-8998-7977
Email: malaysia@happy-science.org
Website: happyscience.org.my

Brazil Headquarters
Rua. Domingos de Morais 1154,
Vila Mariana, Sao Paulo SP
CEP 04009-002, Brazil
Phone: 55-11-5088-3800
Fax: 55-11-5088-3806
Email: sp@happy-science.org
Website: happyscience.com.br

Nepal
Kathmandu Metropolitan City Ward
No. 15,
Ring Road, Kimdol,
Sitapaila Kathmandu, Nepal
Phone: 97-714-272931
Email: nepal@happy-science.org

Jundiai
Rua Congo, 447, Jd. Bonfiglioli
Jundiai-CEP, 13207-340
Phone: 55-11-4587-5952
Email: jundiai@happy-science.org

Uganda
Plot 877 Rubaga Road, Kampala
P.O. Box 34130, Kampala, Uganda
Phone: 256-79-4682-121
Email: uganda@happy-science.org
Website: happyscience-uganda.org

ABOUT IRH PRESS

IRH Press Co., Ltd., based in Tokyo, was founded in 1987 as a publishing division of Happy Science. IRH Press publishes religious and spiritual books, journals, magazines and also operates broadcast and film production enterprises. For more information, visit *okawabooks.com*.

Follow us on:
Facebook: Okawa Books   **Twitter:** Okawa Books
Goodreads: Ryuho Okawa   **Instagram:** OkawaBooks
Pinterest: Okawa Books

--- **NEWSLETTER** ---

To receive book related news, promotions and events, please subscribe to our newsletter below.

https://okawabooks.us11.list-manage.com/subscribe?u=1fc70960eefd92668052ab7f8&id=2fbd8150ef

--- **MEDIA** ---

OKAWA BOOK CLUB

A conversation about Ryuho Okawa's titles, topics ranging from self-help, current affairs, spirituality and religions.

Available at iTunes, Spotify and Amazon Music.

Apple iTunes:
https://podcasts.apple.com/us/podcast/okawa-book-club/id1527893043

Spotify:
https://open.spotify.com/show/09mpgX2iJ6stVm4eBRdo2b

Amazon Music:
https://music.amazon.com/podcasts/7b759f24-ff72-4523-bfee-24f48294998f/Okawa-Book-Club

BOOKS BY RYUHO OKAWA

RYUHO OKAWA'S LAWS SERIES

The Laws Series is an annual volume of books that are mainly comprised of Ryuho Okawa's lectures on various topics that highlight principles and guidelines for the activities of Happy Science every year. *The Laws of the Sun*, the first publication of the laws series, ranked in the annual best-selling list in Japan in 1987. Since then, all of the laws series' titles have ranked in the annual best-selling list for more than two decades, setting socio-cultural trends in Japan and around the world.

The 27th Laws Series
THE LAWS OF SECRET
AWAKEN TO THIS NEW WORLD
AND CHANGE YOUR LIFE

Hardcover • 248 pages • $16.95
ISBN: 978-1-942125-81-5

Our physical world coexists with the multi-dimensional spirit world and we are constantly interacting with some kind of spiritual energy, whether positive or negative, without consciously realizing it. This book reveals how our lives are affected by invisible influences, including the spiritual reasons behind influenza, the novel coronavirus infection, and other illnesses.

The new view of the world in this book will inspire you to change your life in a better direction, and to become someone who can give hope and courage to others in this age of confusion.

For a complete list of books, visit okawabooks.com

THE TRILOGY

The first three volumes of the Laws Series, *The Laws of the Sun*, *The Golden Laws*, and *The Nine Dimensions* make a trilogy that completes the basic framework of the teachings of God's Truths. *The Laws of the Sun* discusses the structure of God's Laws, *The Golden Laws* expounds on the doctrine of time, and *The Nine Dimensions* reveals the nature of space.

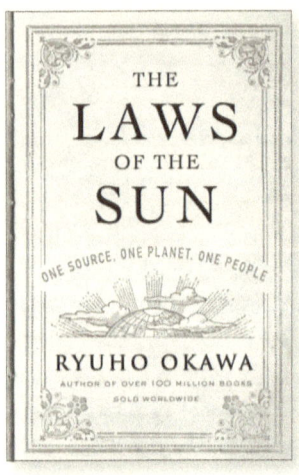

THE LAWS OF THE SUN

ONE SOURCE, ONE PLANET, ONE PEOPLE

Paperback • 288 pages • $15.95
ISBN: 978-1-942125-43-3

IMAGINE IF YOU COULD ASK GOD why He created this world and what spiritual laws He used to shape us—and everything around us. If we could understand His designs and intentions, we could discover what our goals in life should be and whether our actions move us closer to those goals or farther away.

At a young age, a spiritual calling prompted Ryuho Okawa to outline what he innately understood to be universal truths for all humankind. In *The Laws of the Sun*, Okawa outlines these laws of the universe and provides a road map for living one's life with greater purpose and meaning.

In this powerful book, Ryuho Okawa reveals the transcendent nature of consciousness and the secrets of our multidimensional universe and our place in it. By understanding the different stages of love and following the Buddhist Eightfold Path, he believes we can speed up our eternal process of development. *The Laws of the Sun* shows the way to realize true happiness—a happiness that continues from this world through the other.

---

*For a complete list of books, visit **okawabooks.com***

THE GOLDEN LAWS
HISTORY THROUGH THE EYES OF THE ETERNAL BUDDHA

Paperback • 201 pages • $14.95
ISBN: 978-1-941779-81-1

Throughout history, Great Guiding Spirits of Light have been present on Earth in both the East and the West at crucial points in human history to further our spiritual development. *The Golden Laws* reveals how Divine Plan has been unfolding on Earth, and outlines 5,000 years of the secret history of humankind. Once we understand the true course of history, through past, present and into the future, we cannot help but become aware of the significance of our spiritual mission in the present age.

THE NINE DIMENSIONS
UNVEILING THE LAWS OF ETERNITY

Paperback • 168 pages • $15.95
ISBN: 978-0-982698-56-3

This book is a window into the mind of our loving God, who designed this world and the vast, wondrous world of our afterlife as a school with many levels through which our souls learn and grow. When the religions and cultures of the world discover the truth of their common spiritual origin, they will be inspired to accept their differences, come together under faith in God, and build an era of harmony and peaceful progress on Earth.

---

*For a complete list of books, visit **okawabooks.com***

With Savior
Messages from Space Being Yaidron

Paperback • 232 pages • $13.95
ISBN: 978-1-943869-94-7

The human race is now faced with multiple unprecedented crises. Perhaps God is warning us humans to reconsider our materialistic and arrogant ways. Fortunately, God has sent us a savior, who is now teaching us to repent and showing us the path we should choose. In this book, space being Yaidron sends his warnings and messages of hope.

---

*For a complete list of books, visit **okawabooks.com***

THE NOVEL CORONAVIRUS ORIGINATED IN CHINA: LESSONS FOR HUMANKIND

SPIRITUAL MESSAGES FROM SHIBASABURO KITASATO AND R. A. GOAL

Paperback • 228 pages • $13.95
ISBN: 978-1-943869-88-6

This book records spiritual messages from a bacteriologist and a space being. They disclose many truths about the novel coronavirus pandemic, such as China's hidden secrets, what the future holds, and hopeful messages for humanity. Only when humanity learns what we are to learn from this pandemic, can we escape this worldwide crisis and create a new age.

---

*For a complete list of books, visit **okawabooks.com***

BOOKS ON SURVIVING IN THE AGE OF CRISIS

How to Survive the Coronavirus Recession

Paperback • 171 pages • $14.95
ISBN: 978-1-943869-97-8

From the perspectives of both economics and health, this book delves into how you can survive the coronavirus recession. As taught by the author Ryuho Okawa, there is a strong relationship between your spiritual health and immunity, and he demonstrates the mindset you should have as well as introduces a very effective meditation that you can do to truly strengthen your immunity.

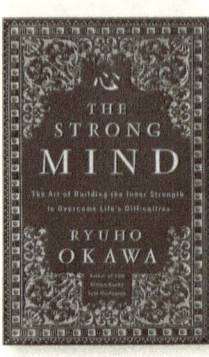

The Strong Mind
The Art of Building the Inner Strength to Overcome Life's Difficulties

Paperback • 192 pages • $15.95
ISBN: 978-1-942125-36-5

The strong mind is what we need to rise time and again, and to move forward no matter what difficulties we face in life. This book will inspire and empower you to take courage, develop a mature and cultivated heart, and achieve resilience and hardiness so that you can break through the barriers of your limits and keep winning in the battle of your life.

The Reason We Are Here
Make Our Powers Together to Realize God's Justice -China Issue, Global Warming, and LGBT-

Paperback • 215 pages • $14.95
ISBN: 978-1-943869-62-6

The Reason We Are Here is a book of thought that is unlike any other: its global perspective, timely opinion on current issues, and spiritual class are unmatched. The main content is the lecture in Toronto, Canada given in October 2019 by Ryuho Okawa, a Japanese spiritual leader and the national teacher of Japan.

For a complete list of books, visit **okawabooks.com**

Inside the Mind of President Biden
Thoughts Revealed by His Guardian Spirit Days before His Inauguration

Paperback • 296 pages • $13.95
ISBN: 978-1-943928-02-6

What are the real thoughts inside the mind of President Biden? What scheme does he know about the coronavirus crisis and the Obama administration's close ties with Beijing? You'll discover whether he can truly fulfill the responsibilities of an American president and a major world leader and also about the way he views the battle between democracy and totalitarianism we are now witnessing.

Spiritual Interviews with the Guardian Spirits of Biden and Trump

Paperback • 200 pages • $11.95
ISBN: 978-1-943869-92-3

The 2020 U.S. presidential election will be a turning point in history. In this book, we spiritually closed in on the true thoughts of Biden and Trump to get a forecast of the presidential election. In short, China could become the next hegemonic state if Biden is elected the president. Who you vote for could change people's lives, for better or worse.

On Carbon Footprints Reducing
Why Greta Gets Angry?

Paperback • 135 pages • $11.95
ISBN: 978-1-943869-59-6

Greta Thunberg, a 16-year-old environmental activist from Sweden, gave a speech at the United Nations Climate Actions Summit that shocked the world in September 2019. In this book, Okawa summons the spiritual beings who have influence on Greta, and has them speak their true intention as to why they made her say what she said.

---

*For a complete list of books, visit **okawabooks.com***

BOOKS ON THE NOVEL CORONAVIRUS INFECTION, THE FUTURE PREDICTION TO HUMANKIND

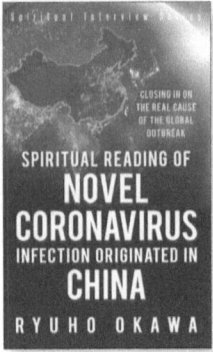

SPIRITUAL READING OF NOVEL CORONAVIRUS INFECTION ORIGINATED IN CHINA
CLOSING IN ON THE REAL CAUSE OF THE GLOBAL OUTBREAK

Paperback • 278 pages • $13.95
ISBN: 978-1-943869-77-0

This worldwide pandemic is not a mere act of nature nor a coincidence, but rather, heaven's warning to humanity, especially China. Through this book, you can find out "the immunity" against the novel coronavirus, among other shocking truths.

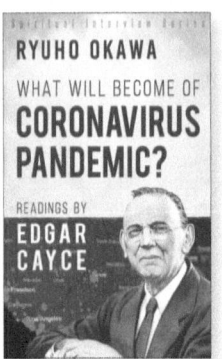

WHAT WILL BECOME OF CORONAVIRUS PANDEMIC?
READINGS BY EDGAR CAYCE

Paperback • 86 pages • $9.95
ISBN: 978-1-943869-82-4

Edgar Cayce, now a spirit in heaven, tells us that the novel coronavirus infection is likely to spread even further, but he also teaches us the truth behind it and how to deal with it. But you, yourself, can gain the power to defeat the novel coronavirus. Here is your light of hope.

SHAKYAMUNI BUDDHA'S FUTURE PREDICTION

Paperback • 213 pages • $13.95
ISBN: 978-1-943869-91-6

In this book, the spirits of Shakyamuni Buddha and John Lennon warn us about the troubles that await humankind, require us who live today to reflect on the arrogance of belittling God, and teach us how to overcome difficulties. What the world needs now are many people who work as a part of God's power. You, too, can become a part of the power to save the world.

*For a complete list of books, visit **okawabooks.com***

BOOKS ON THE TRUTH OF THE SPIRIT WORLD

THE POSSESSION
KNOW THE GHOST CONDITION AND
OVERCOME NEGATIVE SPIRITUAL INFLUENCE

Paperback • 114 pages • $14.95
ISBN: 978-1-943869-66-4

Possession is neither an exceptional occurrence nor unscientific superstition; it's a phenomenon, based on spiritual principles, that is still quite common in the modern society. Through this book, you can find the way to change your own mind and free yourself from possession, and the way to exorcise devils by relying on the power of angels and God.

HEALING FROM WITHIN
LIFE-CHANGING KEYS TO CALM, SPIRITUAL,
AND HEALTHY LIVING

Paperback • 208 pages • $15.95
ISBN:978-1-942125-18-1

None of us wants to become sick, but why is it that we can't avoid illness in life? Is there a meaning behind illness? In this book, author Ryuho Okawa reveals the true causes and remedies for various illnesses that modern medicine doesn't know how to heal. Building a happier and healthier life starts with believing in the power of our mind and understanding the relationship between mind and body.

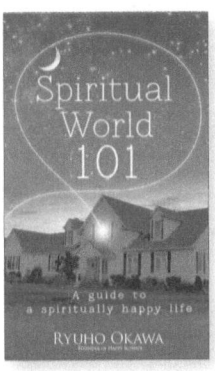

SPIRITUAL WORLD 101
A GUIDE TO A SPIRITUALLY HAPPY LIFE

Paperback • 184 pages • $14.95
ISBN: 978-1-941779-43-9

This book is a spiritual guidebook that will answer all your questions about the spiritual world, with illustrations and diagrams explaining about your guardian spirit and the secrets of God and Buddha. By reading this book, you will be able to understand the true meaning of life and find happiness in everyday life.

---

*For a complete list of books, visit **okawabooks.com***

THE TRUE EIGHTFOLD PATH
Guideposts for Self-Innovation

THE LAWS OF HOPE
The Light is Here

THE HELL YOU NEVER KNEW
and How to Avoid Going There

WORRY-FREE LIVING
Let Go of Stress and Live in Peace and Happiness

UFOS CAUGHT ON CAMERA!
A Spiritual Investigation on Videos and Photos
of the Luminous Objects Visiting Earth

THE REAL EXORCIST
Attain Wisdom to Conquer Evil

THINK BIG!
Be Positive and Be Brave to Achieve Your Dreams

CHANGE YOUR LIFE, CHANGE THE WORLD
A Spiritual Guide to Living Now

INVITATION TO HAPPINESS
7 Inspirations from Your Inner Angel

For a complete list of books, visit **okawabooks.com**

MUSIC BY RYUHO OKAWA

— THE THUNDER —
a composition for repelling the Coronavirus

We have been granted this music from our Lord. It will repel away the novel Coronavirus originated in China. Experience this magnificent powerful music.

Search on YouTube

> the thunder coronavirus 🔍   for a short ad!

— THE EXORCISM —
prayer music for repelling Lost Spirits

Feel the divine vibrations of this Japanese and Western exorcising symphony to banish all evil possessions you suffer from and to purify your space!

Search on YouTube

> the exorcism repelling 🔍   for a short ad!

 Available online
Spotify **iTunes** **Amazon**

CD available at Happy Science local branches and shoja (temples)

WITH SAVIOR

English version

**"Come what may,
you shall expect your future"**

This is the message of hope to the modern people who are living in the midst of the Coronavirus pandemic, natural disasters, economic depression, and other various crises.

Search on YouTube [with savior] for a short ad!

THE WATER REVOLUTION

English and Chinese version

"Power to the People!"

For the truth and happiness of the 1.4 billion people in China who have no freedom. Love, justice, and sacred rage of God are on this melody that will give you courage to fight to bring peace.

Search on YouTube [the water revolution] for a short ad!

From MAY

CD available at Happy Science local branches and shoja (temples)

 Available online
Spotify **iTunes** **Amazon**

www.ingramcontent.com/pod-product-compliance
Lightning Source LLC
Chambersburg PA
CBHW030153100526
44592CB00009B/262